OF HAUNTED SPACES

NTU CENTRE FOR
CONTEMPORARY
ART SINGAPORE

The Films of Ella Raidel

T0345685

Cinema, Heterotopias, And China's Hyperurbanization

Edited by Ute Meta Bauer

Unfolding the Cinematic Real:

The Films of Ella Raidel

——Ute Meta Bauer

Ella Raidel's films are a hybrid of essay documentaries and fiction films, positioned to reveal the fabrication of reality on an individual and social level. Conducting extensive field trips, she has been traveling over the past two decades from Austria to China, and from China to Africa, to investigate China's global expansion through its infrastructural and real estate sectors, revealing the secret path of transitional economic-libidinal flow. Raidel constructs narratives that are synonymous with spaces created through social-cultural capitals on a planetary scale and her films can hence be referred to as 'reality fictions'.

Raidel's recent films illustrate the transformation of rural landscapes into vast urban areas made of steel and concrete, in which she situates characters embodying fairytale desires witnessing these sites' development. In pursuit of a cinematic reality, Raidel blurs the line between fact and fiction by inserting stories of individual characters into these spaces, as her protagonists navigate between their real-life experiences and fantasies. She discovers these narratives in psycho-spatial folds between door frames, mirrors, and newly constructed high-rises, as old ruins decay over time into forgotten memories and ghostly afterimages.[1] Her film characters play diverse and manifold roles, representing today's flexible personalities shaped by neo-liberal modes of production. The inserted small stories unfold how the ideological apparatus creates 'realities' observed by the filmmaker and actors alike, while the invented fictionality serves to indicate the reflexive dimension of filmmaking.

Visiting Mozambique for the first time — a new frontier of contested globalization — she witnessed the effects of an economic treaty that promised new infrastructure in exchange for raw materials. New constructions such as government buildings, airports, bridges, and even a football stadium were inserted into the ecological surroundings. While working on her film *SUBVERSES China in Mozambique* (2011), she was surprised to hear that Hallstatt, a popular tourist town and UNESCO world heritage site near her hometown in Austria, had been copied in China. This became the point of departure for her next film, *Double Happiness* (2014), which gave rise to a transnational story. The film not only addressed today's globalized realities but also pointed out that this copy of a real town was scripted like a film plot, both of which correspond to the fictionality of the current

world economy, molded after the uniform and international style of Western modernity.[2]

Real estate advertisements today do not sell homes to live in. Instead, they promote dreams and fantasies built out of concrete, ready to accumulate as a form of capital flow driven by government-manufactured co-opted desire. After reading a curious note in a local Austrian newspaper reporting that a hotel owner in Hallstatt had discovered that one of her guests was an architect who had been working on the blueprint of Hallstatt's exact replica for five years, Raidel decided to follow up on the story. She found out that the Hallstatt copy had already been built in Boluo, Guangdong Province, and is called Hallstatt See.

In her film *Double Happiness* (2014), which takes its name from the Chinese expression for marriage, Raidel explores the absurdity of this built reality through a play of fiction and reality. In fact, the Chinese Hallstatt See is used as a film set for Korean soap operas and serves as the perfect backdrop for staged wedding pictures in this idyllic Alpine village on a lake. Despite being a copy of the original village, Hallstatt See has not made the real Hallstatt in Austria obsolete. Quite the opposite, the original village, which is a popular destination for Asian tourists, enjoys even greater prosperity due to its 'doppelganger' in China. This double happiness, as the title of the film suggests, is an ironic twist that captures the essence of globalized realities.

In Raidel's *A Pile of Ghosts* (2021), the intersection of hotel ruin owner Charles' obsession with the film *Waterloo Bridge* (1940) and the demolition of his Swallow Hotel becomes a site for exploring themes of nostalgia and memory in a rapidly changing urban landscape. As Charles morphs into the film's male protagonist Roy, played by Robert Taylor in the Hollywood romance, and even adapts Roy's dress code while reciting the latter's lines from the original film, the line between reality and fiction becomes increasingly obscure. This suggests that personal identity is not a fixed entity but rather a flexible construct shaped by individual experiences and cultural production. The film serves as a poignant reminder of the impermanence of physical structures and the intangible yet enduring power of memory and imagination.

The ruin of the Swallow Hotel becomes the stage for Raidel's cinematic excursion. It is the last building standing in a field of architectural fragments on the verge of final demolition, as the sounds of the bulldozers vibrate and reverberate. The place serves as a rare memory of another time and space, a waterloo itself, that will soon only exist as a ghostly photogene.

In this way, Raidel's films become memory theaters, sites of recollection and reflection, where past and present, fact and fiction, reality, and imagination, all intersect and overlap. Her use of amateur actors, as well as her incorporation of real-life locations and situations, fabricate a sense of heightened authenticity and immediacy. Through this approach, Raidel is able to explore complex social and cultural issues in a way that is engaging and thought-provoking, offering a unique perspective on the complexities and conditions of our globalized way of life. Her films serve as a reminder that the stories we tell ourselves about the world around us are always shaped by the cultural, historical, and social contexts into which they are inscribed, and that our experience of reality is always subjective and constructed.

Through a series of texts, this publication aims to unpack the complexity embedded in Raidel's cinematic journeys into the fictional real. In her essay "The Poetry of Haunted Spaces," the architect and urban theorist Marlene Rutzendorfer describes Raidel's films as documentary melodramas that form their own syntax of architectural filmmaking, going beyond the description of spaces or tracing the history of the built environment. What may seem artificial or fabricated belongs to the reality of today's urban fabric. The city, as a psychogeography, as coined by the late artist and situationist Constant Nieuwenhuys, has inscribed narratives.

In my interview with Raidel, we discuss the practice of situated cinema, the development of her projects, and her two-decade long process of making films. Situated knowledge involves producing knowledge that is embedded in genuine historical, cultural, and linguistic contexts. The performativity in her cinematic scenarios transforms individual identification into a collective encounter. The potential of the cinematic experience that Raidel provides lies in the revelation that what is private is public and, therefore indeed, political. These ideas

are inherently inscribed into the apparatus of image-creation and production, from the cinematic and televised images to social media.

The postcolonial theorist Itty Abraham takes the 'China Dream,' a vision of doubt rather than confidence, as the starting point for his text "Double Vision: China from the Outside-In" to discuss Raidel's films as 'moving commentaries'. This helps us to see and hear, in the sonic space of the construction sites, that China is slipping away, leaving behind the absence of a remembered past filled with futures borrowed from other places. He describes her films as human ruins, spaces of ghosts inhabiting a spirit world outlined in the debris of construction.

Hong Kong-based curator and writer Yu Weiying, in her essay "Ghost Infrastructureality," explores the reconfigured Chinese ghost cities as performative entities and maps out the idea of 'ghost infrastructureality.' With reference to Raidel's film *A Pile of Ghosts* (2021), her text is concerned with the infrastructural spatial products created by an urban reality that is speculatively haunted by a seemingly promising yet unfulfilling future based on global capital. For Yu, A Pile of Ghosts presents a planetary perspective on urban infrastructure within the global expansion of built environments that materialize in empty spaces, accumulating a non-productive reality.

These diverse texts collectively uncover the complexity of Raidel's cinematic explorations, accompanied by photographs and stills from her field work and film shoots, which indicate an alternative worldview. Her fictional imagery is embedded in the mundane and repetitive exercises of reality, as if the camera were rehearsing actions with her actors. Only the magical power of cinematic techniques allows one to move in and out of these spatial folds with ease. Ultimately, this publication, with its included images, texts, and on- and off-screen realities, can take our readers on a wild and kaleidoscopic cinematic expedition of their own.

NOTES

1   The folding of cinematic images is treated here as the spatial configuration, the autonomy of the interiorization, in Baroque architecture.
      Gilles Deleuze, *The Fold: Leibniz and the Baroque*, trans. Tom Conley (London: Athlone Press, 1993), 28-29.
2   Norman M. Klein, *The Vatican to Vegas: The History of Special Effects* (New York: The New Press, 2004), 321.

The Films

The Seven-Step Verse
A Pile of Ghosts
We'll Always Have Paris
Double Happiness
Subverses:
     China in Mozambique
Cinema Isn't I See, It's I Fly
Play Life Series
SLAM VIDEO MAPUTO

The Seven-Step Verse

VR, 9 min, 2022

This cinematic VR work explores the relationship between work, body, and space in Singapore's iconic modernist shopping malls in the post-pandemic times. As the performers intervene these malls, they appropriate clothing and gestures, while also reciting texts as they pass by — thus gesturing towards the underlying ideological hierarchy embedded in the very concrete of these social structures. These commercial buildings, once monuments of rapid urbanization, have nowadays been reconfigured for a new clientele consisting largely of female domestic helpers from neighboring Southeast Asian countries. *The Seven-Step Verse* is inspired by the Chinese poet Cao Zhi, who composed a poem in seven footsteps and demonstrated his literary genius with the subject of intimate comradeship. By applying the literary methods of reciting the texts in these malls to compose a poem of *object trouvé*, the film traverses the mind, pedestrians, and the everyday random encounter to narrate the urban space that encapsulates the invisibility of the personal lives of domestic caretakers.

A Pile of Ghosts

70 min, 2021

Based on a true story of a dandyesque nail house owner, Charles, the film tells a romantic ghost story of China's urbanization through his fantasy of being the actor in the Hollywood classic, *Waterloo Bridge* (1940) — a film which was regarded in China as one of the early signs of Westernization. The Swallow Hotel, which Charles inherited from his parents, still stands in the hilly urban space of Chongqing as a relic, decorated with idiosyncratic ornaments from the past regime. Resisting gentrification, Charles becomes a lone hero against the speculative economy, which transforms living space, histories, and memory. As he gradually retreats into his phantasmagorical experience, the actress of *Waterloo Bridge* comes alive to linger with him in the ever-changing urban scenes of Chongqing.

In reference to the Chinese classic ghost story, *A Pile of Ghosts in West Mountain* (西山一窟鬼, *Xi Shan Yi Ku Gui*), the spectral effect of global capitalism fosters the dialogue between reality and the imagination as it navigates between living and life, appearance and existence, as well as film and fiction. The vexing interplay of documentary and fiction, in which construction workers, investors, and real estate agents appear, takes place in contemporary China, where cities are built entirely on speculation as individual characters are dictated by the invisible strings of capitalism in every move. From the romantic melody of the movie theme, Auld Lang Syne, to Gangnam-style electronic music, the reality, at the same time, turns out to be increasingly porous.

We Will Always Have Paris

4 min, 2020

The Eiffel Tower, Champs-Élysées, magnificent fountains, and trimmed hedges stand as faux French in the hazy rain of Tianducheng. The residential complex located in the suburbs of the Chinese megapolis, Hangzhou, is one of the countless, largely unpopulated pop-up sites that sprang up overnight through high-speed real-estate speculation. In Raidel's film, the Eiffel Tower becomes the anti-gravity center of a phantom zone furnished with stark high-rises, parking areas, and gardens — an urban proposition that amounts \to nothing. As a nod to Hollywood Classics, *Casablanca* (1942), the appropriated title from the dialogue of the film alludes to a fleeting romance of global urbanization that later turns ghostly, |as the stress breathes to fog up the glasses and inscribes the sentence, "I have been here."

Double Happiness

74 min, 2014

A replica of the idyllic Austrian village, Hallstatt, standing in Guangdong, China, poses the question of cultural translation, simulation, and fantasy in the global political economy. In the fashion of a docu-musical where singing and dancing become the predominant mode of narration, the film's references to *The Sound of Music* (1965), the Hollywood production of a fantasized Austrian culture, is re-enacted. The musical performances in a pastoral landscape remind us of the identity politics in the global system, and how fantasy traverses the ideal of living through mediated realities. China's Hallstatt See in Boluo was planned as a residential area and was later turned into a contemporary theme park within only one year. Meanwhile, the original Hallstatt had already been the shooting scene for Japanese and Korean soaps and boosted tourism from Asia to Austria.

The title, *Double Happiness*, refers to the happiness that increases twofold in marriage. The written character 喜 (happiness, *xi*) is doubled as 囍 , where in other words, *Double Happiness* is a happiness that simulates each other. The etymology of the Chinese word is taken as the allegory of cultural translation in its fusing of different traditions and histories into a romance of our times, which are mediated by the political economy and the collective desire.

Subverses: China in Mozambique

45 min, 2011

Raidel's *Subverse: China in Mozambique* depicts Chinese and Mozambican laborers and their working conditions in China's growing engagement in infrastructure projects. Taking the memos of |an anonymous Chinese worker as the source of the main narrative, the film is punctuated with commentaries done in local Mozambican slam poetry, which not only indicates the presence of subcultures in flux around the world, but also serves as an oral tradition that utters the truth of the event. The working conditions of these workers in plight are stratified by the socio-economic relations of the difference of colors and cultures, trafficked |in the flow of capital. In the wave of globalization, the process of eliminating and reconstructing boundaries triggers mutual conflicts and struggles for power relations between local and distant cultures. The disoriented ethnic conflicts in the film bring to light the uneven phenomenon of globalization and transcontinental modernity.

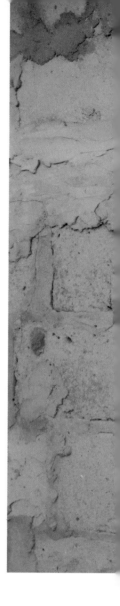

Cinema Isn't I See, It's I Fly

1 min, 2013

In homage to Soviet filmmaker and theorist Dziga Vertov in terms of the ontology of cinema, Raidel creates a tongue-in-cheek performative sequence in Taipei's local hardware store. With the melody of a telephone ringtone the camera zooms into the store owner's TV monitor, showing an image of a parachuting skydiver, the director's brother. The global vision of the mediated *mise en abyme* propels us into worlding of vertiginous perceptions.

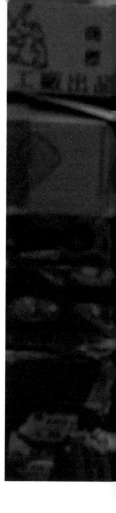

Play Life Series

11 min, 2012

Raidel's work deals ironically with the Chinese soap opera as a fake factory of collective desires, which, in the interplay of fiction and the making of it, forces its way through reality and scrutinizes it as a site of image-making and image-controlling.

In *Play Life Series*, an enchanted examination of image production in China's film and TV studio is presented through repetitive rehearsals looped between art and life. In Mandarin, "Play Life" (*wan ming*) not only means risking one's life or a desperate move for pursuing something worthwhile, but also an attitude towards life as a theatrical play though cameras continuously rehearse the social ideology that lurks in exercise of image production. There are three episodes: "Play Life Hit" depicts two Chinese sword fighters swirling in the air, tightened by steel cables as in any Wuxia film such as *Crouching Tiger, Hidden Dragon* (2000); "Play Life Cry" features a nervous job interviewee crying and holding Mao's Red Book to demonstrate her relentless loyalty to the company as indicative of the perverted communist capitalism in China; and "Play Life Love" involves a heartbroken young woman mindlessly drifting along the streets to cheesy pop music much like a predictable and stereotypical setting in any Asian soap. Always showing what is in front of cameras and even behind them, *Play Life Series* makes the making-of of image production transparent, which virtually circulates in social space, both fiction and real.

SLAM VIDEO MAPUTO

27 min, 2010

The work addresses issues of perception and of the strategies of self-analysis in Afro-pop music and image production through the reflexive disclosing of the fabrication of music videos in Maputo, Mozambique. Africa's musical roots travel around the world to return to Africa in full circle in the guise of gangsta rap, hip hop, reggae, dub, and so on. Raidel's imagery on the production of music videos is situated in a global current that spans the gap between the glamor of this particular business and the realities of Africa—the plightful economic and social realities of the seedbed of music culture.

The Poetry of Haunted Spaces: Ella Raidel and the Documentary Melodrama

——Marlene Rutzendorfer

A mountain range. Scarce vegetation. Blue skies and the chirping of crickets. A bird here and there. Then the song sets in, tenderly hummed. The fragile human voice stands in contrast with the rocky landscape that seems to have been there forever. Or is it the landscape that is instead fragile? Is it, in fact, the glacier — appearing in the distance — that is about to disappear forever? The voice pauses, takes its time, then carries us through to the title of the film: 雙喜 *Double Happiness*.

When the popular Chinese folk song *Mo Li Hua* (Jasmine Flower) sets the mood for a scene in Ella Raidel's *Double Happiness* (2014), the poetry of spaces haunted by the ghosts of multiple eras accompanies its setting. In the opening scene of the film, the sound and landscape create a hybrid place that is neither defined nor delineated in space and time. Instead it becomes a speculative place in and of itself, a series of sequences that could, indeed, form a montage of various sites — a collage of sight and sound. Within a few cadres, Raidel lays bare the artificiality and vulnerability embedded in the cultural appropriation of a landscape. However, this is not a *Heimatfilm*. In fact, home is a concept as elusive as a fleeting tune in Raidel's films.

Consistently in dialogue with Chinese independent cinema, Raidel conveys a multiplicity of layers of meaning and sociopolitical messages in the film's soundscape, in turn evoking memories and sentiments that go beyond a mere pop cultural reference or the entertainment value of a well sung melody. *Mo Li Hua* is, after all, more than a love song. For generations of Chinese, it has evoked an era of cultural opening and change and has unraveled their lived realities in the aftermath of the Cultural Revolution. In *Double Happiness*, we encounter the melody in multiple forms, each of them carrying a notion of cultural hybridity. Duplicity and mirage appear and reappear in Raidel's films. *Double Happiness* plays with uncertainties created by the doubling of a millennia-old salt mining town by lake Hallstatt in the shape of an urban development project near Shenzhen, a former fishing village-turned-production hub and megapolis within only a few decades. The protagonist performs *Mo Li Hua* in a Dirndl on the replicated main square of Hallstatt, while the Salinen Quintet Hallstatt performs the melody at an official ceremony in Shenzhen. It is with this that the film moves between the perceived factuality of documentary cinema, the verve and irony of a musical comedy, and the sentiment of a melodrama.

This play with fictionality, music, and layers of representation takes center stage when actress Yaki Cang addresses the camera, while the sparkle of her cocktail dress melds in with the city lights and the full moon, and she sings the words made famous by Teresa Teng:[1]

月亮代表我的心	*The Moon Represents My Heart*
你问我爱你有多深	You ask me how deep my love is for you,
我爱你有几分	How much I really love you.
我的情也真	My affection is real,
我的爱也真	My love is real,
月亮代表我的心	The moon represents my heart.
轻轻的一个吻	Just one soft kiss
已经打动我的心	Is enough to move my heart.
深深的一段情	A period of time when our affection was deep,
教我思念到如今	Has made me miss you until now.

Is this a love song for a person or a city? Is it an attempt at exhausting a place's collective memory, while the city seems to be fixated on economic and urban growth, while being on the move?

This emotional and physical exhaustion also forms an underlying theme in *A Pile of Ghosts*. Again, Raidel turns to the poetry of another Taiwanese singer You Ya.[2] Here, it is not the cityscape of Shenzhen that You Ya's song seems to address but the exploitation of resources and land in the oil field. In this sequence, the montage of image and sound moves swiftly from a pair of distanced lovers — or close strangers — in a hotel room to an undefined, industrial noise that may very well come from the construction site surrounding the hotel they are in. A sudden cut, however, takes us to the red earth of an industrial environment and brings us closer to the acoustic source. Where have we heard this noise before? The rhythmic sound seems familiar, and the scene is suddenly reminiscent of the famous opening of *Once Upon a Time in the West* (1968). But before we can settle on that, the sound and image slowly find each other, and we discern oil pumps, working and exhausting the reserves of an otherwise scarce landscape.

Just one soft
kiss is enough to
move my heart.
A period of
time when our
affection was deep,
has made me
miss you until now.

"We'll always have Paris," Rick Blaine (Humphrey Bogart) says to Ilsa Lund (Ingrid Bergman) before they part ways on a foggy night at the airport in Michael Curtiz' *Casablanca* (1942). We'll always have Paris is also the title of Ella Raidel's short film set in a foggy and rainy Tianducheng, a housing development reminiscent of Haussmannian Paris. Raidel transposes this legendary quote from a Hollywood melodrama to a context of urban renewal, where the vacancy of monumental buildings and newly developed cities summons the possibilities that have so often become the driving force in the speculative documentary language she has developed over the years. As an outsider, reflecting on her own otherness, Raidel finds poetry in the state of the in-between: the in-between of eras, the in-between of stages, the in-between of urban development, and the not-yet that follows the no-longer. In doing so, Raidel forms a palimpsest with the stories that have unfolded in an urban space, in dwellings, and in the social fabric of the city; this state in limbo then becomes a creative space for performers that improvise in the cadres that the trained photographer and cinematographer opens for them, like a playground. Here, a stage emerges within the urban fabric — a world of fabulating futures and potentialities, in which the actors are indeed agents that direct the flow of the story that unfolds. The filmic space becomes a phantasmagorical space, and like Walter Benjamin's flâneur wandering and wondering through the rapid changes of Haussmannian Paris, the filmmaker-flâneuse accompanies unscripted scenes between performers in a scripted setting through a palimpsest of drafts, rubble, dreams, and ghosts from lives lived in the past.

Here, the doubling of space not only happens in the actual re-construction and adaptation of famed architectural models such as the Egyptian Sphinx or the Eiffel Tower — this doubling also unfolds on screen and reflects on the role of filmmaking itself and on the impossibilities of documentary cinema. Raidel provokes reality. "A documentary film is produced largely in the montage," she tells me in a conversation in preparation of this publication. Her decision to render the artificiality of the process visible in a Brechtian *Verfremdungseffekt* [alienation effect] takes shape in the process of performativity and the actors' improvisation of multiple roles, as well as the aesthetics and linguistics of TV ads for real estate projects. These effects create an awareness of the woman behind the movie

You are about to change your heart. Just like time that can't be turned back. I can only embrace you in dreams.

camera, which often — quite ironically — manages to convey more of the lived experience than a traditional talking-heads-voice-over-documentary-format is capable of.

Raidel may not be the first to work with performative elements in documentary filmmaking. However, with her overlapping of place, narrative, and time, and her understanding of the city and urban space as an active character in what I would call documentary melodramas, she forms her own syntax of architectural filmmaking that goes beyond a mere portrait of a space or the tracing of a built environment's history. It deals with the past, present, and future, as well as with the possibilities that never actually materialize lingering on in the atmosphere and landscape of haunted spaces. At the same time, this interplay between reality and potentiality becomes a guessing game in which the viewer's expectations are all too often proven wrong. In *A Pile of Ghosts* (2021), for instance, what might seem artificial or fabricated does, in fact, belong to the urban fabric, such as the repeated sound and vision scape of *Waterloo Bridge* (1940), a black and white World War II melodrama starring Vivian Leigh, which is playing on the TV set of a partially abandoned hotel.

What is not left to chance or improvisation, though, is the cadre — the frame of each scene that is meticulously planned and carried out. In a scene from *A Pile of Ghosts*, in which the grayness of a construction site evokes the aesthetics of black and white cinema, our understanding of colors and the depth or flatness of a space is abruptly broken when a construction worker enters the frame in bright orange overalls. This is an outfit and visual code that is later taken up by Charles Yang, owner of the hotel and one of the main characters of the film, as he stands in a dimly lit alley, waiting on the cusp of things to come. It is scenes like these, when Raidel's sense of humor and that of the protagonists shines through. Forming a kind of *Verfremdungseffekt* that startles us, we cannot immediately decode the situations we witness and this, in turn, creates friction in the flow of the film. In yet another scene, actor Yaki Cang knocks on the door of Charles' hotel and claims to have booked a room online in a place that does not seem to be able to physically withstand the test of time — or of urban renewal — for much longer. The place and its owner seem to dwell in the past — or do they, in fact, represent a potential future in a surrounding landscape of high-rise buildings that are the result of failed (post-) modern urban planning?

This begs the question of who has, indeed, a right to the commodified city. Raidel's exploration of fictionalization and play is reminiscent of what Henri Lefebvre wrote in the essay of the same title, discussing "the need for creative activity, for the *oeuvre* (not only of products and consumable material goods), of the need for information, symbolism, the imaginary and play."[3] By appropriating dilapidated spaces and construction sites that undergo a state of transformation, protagonists Charles Yang and Yaki Cang counter hegemonial urban practices, hence writing a counter narrative of the city. In his decision to stay in the hotel, Yang is, in a way, practicing a counter performance of the city. Again, the in-between comes to mind. This practice recalls Homi Bhabha's notion of the (...) contingent 'in-between' space, that innovates and interrupts the performance of the present. The 'past-present' becomes part of the necessity, not the nostalgia, of living."[4] Is this, in fact, a different kind of 'newness'[5] in opposition to the one we encounter in the ongoing top-down urban renewal process changing not only the material but also the social fabric of the city? Is this the poetry of rewriting the city?

Charles and Yaki are not the only protagonists in Ella's films that share this form of poetry. Poetry functioning as a 'counter hegemonic cultural practice'[6] is also central to the earlier *Slam Video Maputo* (2010) and *SUBVERSES China in Mozambique* (2011). Here, slam poetry serves as a basis and starting point, and becomes a means of subverting the uncertainty of the in-between, a way of unsettling and reassessing power relations within rapidly changing cityscapes, where labor and art lie at the heart of the counter-narrative of a city. The processes of writing, commenting, and performing merge with the space the artists describe in their own texts. And the texts and performances tell stories of the city in a post and neo-colonial setting, addressing the harsh ironies of a late capitalist and late socialist logic of construction and exploitation.

In Raidel's films, laborers, construction workers, and retail assistants repeatedly share their perspectives on the spaces they co create or try to advertise. Their stories actively haunt the shiny facades of the showrooms and empty model apartments and entire districts that have been deserted, evoking an eerie sense of clairvoyance in a world still reeling in the impact of COVID-19 and social distancing.

In a late-capitalist and post-colonial world, the hybridity of space and space production is underlined, with Lefebvre's much cited *Right to the City* questioned and re-affirmed, and the *Location of Culture* re- and de-centered. In this hybrid world we operate in — day in, day out — the urban fabric and the environment under construction create a multitude of narratives and film forms; they formulate spaces that overlap with histories and archaeologies that are not only buried underneath the surface and seem to later pop up in a Freudian way when we least expect or want it, they also appear to hover in mid-air, like cosmic background radiation. Raidel dips into these ghost stories, the poetry, the humor, and the melodrama of contemporary urban life, creating artifacts in her own filmic language that reflect on the human condition in the surreality of a post-modern world.

NOTES

1   Yi Sun, "The Moon Represents My Heart (月亮代表我的心, 1972)" in *Double Happiness* (2014), directed by Ella Raidel, performed by Yaki Cang.

2   Huang Kun Lin and Jia Chang Liu, "The Past Can Only Be Remembered (往事只能回味, 1970)," in *A Pile of Ghosts* (2021), directed by Ella Raidel, performed by Charles Yang.

3   Henri Lefebvre, "The Right to the City," in *Writings on Cities*, ed. and trans. Eleonore Kofman and Elizabeth Lebas (Oxford: Blackwell Publishers, 1996), 147.

4   Homi K. Bhabha, "Locations of Culture," in *The Location of Culture*. (London, UK: Routledge, 2004), 10.

5   Ibid.

6   Bell Hooks, "Choosing the Margins as a Space of Radical Openness," in *Framework: The Journal of Cinema and Media*, no. 36 (1989): 15-23.

There's a magic in the air. Now I see it, now I smell it, now, I feel it. The chance is changing, the chance is causing, the chance is coming, the chance is going, so, don't let it go, 'cause we can't be sure if it's gonna come back around.

Situated Cinema: The City as a Text

——A Conversation between Ute Meta Bauer and Ella Raidel

UMB   You've lived in Asia, more precisely Taiwan, for more than 20 years. During that time, you made three films about China: *SUBVERSES China in Mozambique* (2011) on the Chinese investments in Africa, *Double Happiness* (2014) on the clone of an Austrian Village near Shenzhen, and *A Pile of Ghosts* (2021) on Chinese ghost cities. These films now form a trilogy on China's rapid urbanization and infrastructural expansion — topics of geopolitical significance. What drew you to these topics?

ER   When I visited Taipei two decades ago, I was intrigued by its urban configuration. The city holds layers and traces of tradition, history, and modernization to be understood and uncovered. Like a palimpsest, the city constantly writes over what has been written, built, erased, and reconfigured.

In my time in Taipei, I witnessed how the city expanded over the years, especially on the outskirts. Many high-rise buildings were built, and I came across many advertisements by real estate agencies that promised a fairytale-like experience, like riding horses on the riverside. In reality, nature was increasingly pushed back, and landscapes were morphed to make space for these buildings. And ironically, once these apartments were sold, highways were then built directly in front of them, blocking the picturesque view that has been promised to its buyers.

UMB   This idea of the city as a palimpsest seems to tie in closely with the idea of reading the city as a text. You also mentioned coming across several real estate advertisements — were these integral to the research you were conducting behind the scenes and in the films?

ER   Yes. I collected advertisements and slogans promoting these real estate projects and agencies, and eventually used them in my films as documents of our contemporary times. They reflect how living conditions are bound to a larger social narrative; these texts do not only promote buildings but regulate desire. I've often found that urban space is haunted by the dreams and promises offered by governments, urban planners, and real estate developers.

UMB   And their histories.

ER   Absolutely. Urban space, especially in East and Southeast Asia, is built upon layers of colonial histories that are erased to make space for new imaginations or ideologies. In Taipei, for example, streets are named after cities in Mainland China. In this sense a map of China is imprinted in the logic of the infrastructure, and we can read a city like a socio-political text.

UMB   Indeed, a city like Taipei can be seen as a China imagined. Like you mentioned, there is so much intertextual significance between cities, especially Asian ones. Films tend to invoke the memories embedded in their dense urban fabric — are there any works that you have been inspired by or preoccupied with in your own research?

ER   Yes. Before I moved to Taiwan, I was always interested in how it was like there. I started to watch films from Taiwan — especially films from the Taiwan New Wave. This included works by Edward Yang, Hou Hsiao Hsien, and Tsai Ming Liang.

UMB   If I recall, you've done copious amounts of research on Tsai Ming Liang's work, and you seem to have been mesmerized by it. What kind of impression does his work give you, and how has it inspired you?

ER   I first saw Tsai Ming Liang's *The River* (1997) in Berlin, where I was living at the time, and was taken by the slowness of his cinema. His film opens with a very long shot, where almost nothing happens; you see a father sitting on the kitchen table, smoking a cigarette for an extended period of time. Chantal Akerman's film, *From the East* (1993) had a similar impression on me. For me, such cinematic slowness allows us to meditate on what we are seeing — it opens a space for thought and reflection, with silence in between.

UMB   Would you say that Tsai's films resonate with you possibly because they also reflect life in Taiwan from the point of view of an outsider?

ER   Perhaps. Tsai himself is Chinese Malaysian, i.e. from overseas. He portrays landscapes and urban landscapes amidst rapid urbanization. And his films are dominated by cubical spaces, where protagonists often find themselves trapped and alienated from their environment, just as they are confined by familial expectations and traditions. In his ilms, I see how the city functions as a script that has been pre-written for its inhabitants.

JMB   In many ways, they seem to be prisoners of their own reality. Considering your research on Tsai Ming Liang's films, in what way does Chinese language cinema help you understand the geopolitics of Taiwan, or its history?

ER   With my research on East Asian cinema and my conversations with filmmakers, it was ultimately through the post-colonial experiences of filmmakers in Taiwan that I gained an understanding of the geopolitical context of the region.

UMB   Given the ongoing political tension and cultural differences between Taiwan and China, why did your interest turn to the mainland? What are some of the themes you were interested in when it comes to China?

ER   I was curious about China because of being both so close to Taiwan, geographically, yet so distant at the same time because of the constant political conflict between the two.

I had the opportunity to attend several artist residencies in China. During a residency at During a residency at Red Gate Gallery 2010 on the outskirts of Beijing, whole villages behind the residency were being bulldozed. Every day, I watched whole villages being erased to make space for new urban developments — and driving by these new virgin cities at night, you would see developments that ultimately remain empty. These cities appear like monstrous shadows and ghosts warning us that the incessant shaping and re-shaping of the natural landscape, the sealing of land with concrete mass — urbanization on such a monumental scale — will eventually lead to environmental collapse.

UMB   It wouldn't be difficult to imagine that living in this part of the world and bearing witness to these events would eventually influence the topics of your films and research.

ER   Precisely. I eventually developed my practice as a filmmaker in this environment, in tandem with my research on Chinese language cinema. During my artist residencies in China, I spoke to filmmakers

who were a large part of Chinese independent film culture, such as Zhu Rikun, Wang Bing, Pema Tseden, Wu Wenguang, Mengqi Zhang, and others. It was not only interesting to talk to them, but also being able to witness for myself the cultural shifts and changes that determined their filmmaking. I was mesmerized by how they had to work around censorship and still take a critical stance on what was happening around them, and also found that many of them channel criticism not only through images, but with sounds as a sub-narrative.

MB   Your research and filmmaking are focused on various aspects of urbanization in China, and of fragmentation and displacement. And yet two of your films were shot in Mozambique; *Slam Video Maputo* (2009) and *SUBVERSES China in Mozambique* (2011). Both films are rather unconventional documentaries. How did you discover these topics in Africa and develop your cinematic language?

ER   In 2009, I was invited by Gertjan Zuilhof from the International Film Festival Rotterdam to join a program titled 'Forget Africa'. The aim of the program was to discover and research African filmmakers and foster exchange with international ones. Among the filmmakers he invited were Sherman Ong, Tan Chui Mui, and Jakrawal Nilthamron from East and Southeast Asia, Joanna Vasquez Arong and Uli Schueppel from Europe, and Kimi Takesue and Kevin J. Everson from the US. We embarked on short trips to Sub-Saharan Africa to shoot short films in countries of our choice, and in turn he would invite African filmmakers to go to China. The films of Sherman Ong and Jakrawal Nilthamron were influential for me — they made remarkable hybrid films in-between fiction and documentary in a very short time, and that sparked my interest.

UMB   Could you tell us more about Mozambique, and why you chose to travel to that country in particular?

ER   I had never been to Sub-Saharan Africa, but I had read in the past that Jean-Luc Godard and his wife Anne-Marie Miéville were invited to Maputo in 1978/79 for their *Sonimage* project titled *'The Birth [of an image] of a Nation'*. Godard attempted to give local workshops in filmmaking. I went there to see what was left of the project and eventually shot a short film — *Slam Video Maputo* (2009), where I followed local music video producers to their shooting sites. During this time, I got to

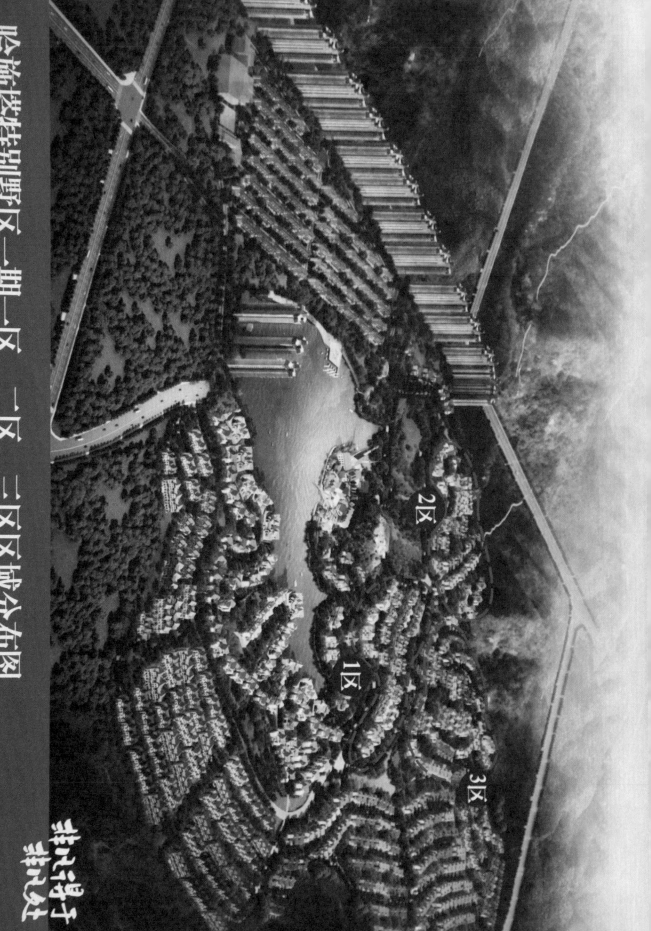

哈施塔特别墅区一期一区、二区、三区区域分布图

2区

1区

3区

know a group of Slam Poets — *Poetas d'Alma* — who were organizing poetry events in the German Goethe Institute. These Slam Poets later became a part of both films, as a sub-verse — an underlying, second narrative, as well as a poetic device.

JMB   And that led you to another film: *SUBVERSES China in Mozambique* (2011). Interestingly, that film focuses on China, although you were shooting in Africa. How did these two geographies merge, and what are 'sub-verses'?

ER   'Sub-verses' is both a play on the word 'verse' — that of the slam poetry being performed — and the subversive effect of its performance, as well as an indirect reference to texts that originate from 'what lies below'. Namely, can the south speak, and how? While working on *Slam Video Maputo* (2009), I saw Chinese construction workers in the streets, whom locals said they were prisoners from China. I later went back on a second visit to research and shoot *SUBVERSES China in Mozambique* (2011). This time, I investigated the economic involvement and presence of China in Africa which manifested itself in infrastructural projects, such as a new airport in Maputo, government buildings, a football stadium, as well as bridges and roads. In this film, I started to include poetry, songs, and letters as sub-verses to the dominant narratives at hand. I combined observational shots and documentation, intersected, and punctuated by performative acts.

JMB   You mentioned 'performative acts', though of course your definition of performativity is likely to be different from the approach of Judith Butler's gender politics or J. L. Austin's linguistic analysis. In what alternative sense are your films performative? What is the idea and motivation behind your performative strategies?

ER   Rather than trying to be informative — I'm not a journalist — I look for sensible forms of expression. On my field trips to China, I no longer just photograph or shoot a site; if possible, I work with actors — players and performers — through re-enactments. My performative strategies arose out of the restrictions I faced, and I developed re-enactments and improvisations as a working method to access locations without permits, and to activate sites with characters. Yakira Cang, who is excellent in her improvisations, was the actress in my films

Double Happiness and *A Pile of Ghosts*. We would go to a site, and she would just stand there or dress up like a worker, a dog owner, a peasant, or a real estate lady. For example, she would walk around looking for her dog, and this would become a scene in the film.

UMB   Would this serve as a part of the 'sub-verses' you were speaking of earlier?

ER   Yes. The focus, of course, was not on her nor the missing dog, but instead on the sub-verses — the villages in the background being torn down for new developments. These areas were covered with green translucent fabric — the safety nets — under which you could still see the old village's structures, and, beneath the rubbish, the belongings of previous residents. Each area was surrounded by a brick wall, and nearby residents would break holes into the wall to access the forbidden area. These holes are like symbols of resistance and freedom, but we don't need to state our findings or interpretations. Instead, with re-enactments and improvisation, we can research the city by walking through it and exploring it — just as Yakira Cang walked through the site looking for her dog.

UMB   The result is that your films exist somewhere between fact and fiction, between documentary and speculation. This interest in hybridity continues in your film *Double Happiness* (2014), about the village of Hallstatt, Austria, and an exact copy of the village replicated in Boluo, China. How did these strategies develop as you address the forces of cultural simulacrum?

ER   The inspiration to copy this village — what the developer calls "the most beautiful village in the world" — is derived not only from its natural beauty, but from the images and sub-verses created around it. The fascination with Austria, for example, stems from *The Sound of Music* (1965), a Hollywood fantasy of Austria. When you visit Hallstatt, you see many Asian tourists dressed up in traditional local costumes posing in front of the houses and the village's monuments — a kind of cosplay for photo-taking opportunities.

UMB   And the same could be said for the copied village in Boluo?

ER   It's somewhat similar — the village in Boluo serves mainly as a backdrop for shooting wedding pictures and soap operas. I was particularly interested in how 'the Hallstatt project' was advertised through architectural plans and models, rendered images, promotional animations, and weddings pictures. These are all part of the image-making and imagination-building processes of a place.

I like to refer to what Hito Steyerl said about "images that cross the screen", that images produced in post-production or photoshop cross the screen to become real images. These are what she refers to as "poor images" like the images of the copied Hallstatt, in which the perspectives are scaled so the village seems out of perspective, or inverted like a mirror-image, as if the image had been flipped in postproduction, perhaps by accident. They remain forever copies, as simulacra par excellence, like low-resolution jpeg-files.

UMB   Images that cross the screen seem to play a rather prominent role in your filmmaking process.

ER   They do. The logic of it led me to play, to traverse, and to transform with images. I stage characters and use songs that all contribute to creating a fantasy or take them apart to be inserted or misplaced in another context, in turn translating them differently. I am very much interested in this form of narrative — let's call it speculative or performative documentary — because the audience constantly needs to navigate the fictionality of the real, and the reality of fiction. My films are models of thought that make you think and labor upon the visual and sonic experience.

UMB   *Double Happiness* (2014) interrogates the collective fantasy surrounding the novel and the foreign. You return to this same tension in your recent work, *A Pile of Ghosts* (2021) that is also situated in China — the result of your research project titled *Of Haunted Spaces*. This investigation was also important for the development of your script. What is *Of Haunted Spaces* about? How do spaces come to be haunted, and what kind of ghosts do they address?

ER   *Of Haunted Spaces* is a natural extension of my interest in urbanization and infrastructural projects from and in China. My field research included visiting many ghost cities all over China, such as the

abandoned holiday resorts on the east coast of Shandong Province, or New Lanzhou Area in the west, where hundreds of mountains in Gansu Province had been flattened to build a new city. Each of these newly developed areas has a theme park to promote the area, and they include replications of other parts of the world — such as the Sphinx and the Acropolis in Lanzhou New Area. However, now they are abandoned spectacles of ruination. They are uninhabited sites haunted by surplus production and financial speculation fueled by global capitalism.

UMB   How did you approach these spaces in order to conjure up these ghosts, then? Was your method of research and filmmaking also performative in this instance?

ER   My field research naturally became a part of my filmmaking process. While researching these ghost cities, I was looking for protagonists who could express these drastic changes. In one of my visits to Chongqing, I was introduced to Charles, the owner of a "nail house", the colloquial term for the last house in an area to get torn down. Charles resides in the ruins of the Swallow Hotel, situated in the hillside of Chongqing, and once run by him and his family. He refuses to move although everyone around him has left. And while resisting government control for years, he became an actor.

UMB   Could you tell us more about the Swallow Hotel, as well as your experience working with Charles as a performer?

ER   When I first entered his house, he was watching *Waterloo Bridge* (1940) and I realized he was dressed like the main character, Roy (Robert Taylor) in the film. The setup of his hotel and his personality were perfect for making a film, since Charles was the transfiguration of Roy, who also symbolizes China's westernization and capitalization. These details are not invented, and Charles really seemed to be morphing into a fictional character. From there, I gave him a story about a female ghost, Mira (Vivian Leigh), who appears in front of him and speaks lines adapted from the original Hollywood movie. In the story, he searches for Mira, who incidentally sounds like a mirage — an illusion, or a ghost.

UMB   Did you attempt the improvisation with Charles in the same way as with Yakira Cang?

ER   We did take on an approach of improvisation, but it wasn't necessarily the same as with Yakira Cang. We went out onto the streets and visited a doctor, a shoemaker, a TV repairman and so on. Charles presented them with his ghost story, and we improvised on it, with very funny effects. I visited Charles over three years, and we repeated scenes. Each time, the ruination of the place and the urban development of Chongqing intensified, and we all grew older, which you can see in the film. On each visit, the story grew richer. It was like we were playing our own lives through the course of the film and improvising as we went along. These are more than performances — they are performative acts. We are not only acting out the social script that governs how people behave in reality, but improvise from and with it, as we play with the site, situation, and fiction.

UMB   Your film takes references from classic Hollywood films such as *Waterloo Bridge* (1940) or *Casablanca* (1942) and western dress styles, as well as the physical changes and cultural transitions that are happening in China. That speaks to the diversity of the viewers as well: Today's audience, after all, cannot be homogeneously composed. Who do you imagine to constitute your audience and how do you address it? How do viewers in Asia react to this film, versus those from Europe, for example?

ER   I believe I have two audiences that see different aspects in this film. There is the European or Western audience who is curious about China, and then there is the Chinese or Asian audience that recognize in this film songs which have historical allusions and significance. Certain songs and films were popular at a time when China was opening up to the West, and references to these songs and films later became symbols of change. I believe that we can address both audiences with different layers of references, even if they cannot be homogeneously composed.

UMB   Your latest work The Seven Step Verse (2022) is a cinematic Virtual Reality (VR) film. What is a 'Seven Step Verse'? Can you explain what the title refers to?

ER   The title The Seven Step Verse emerges from an obsession with the number seven, which has a special meaning. As I was looking for

a title that included the number seven, I came across the poet Cao Zhi's "The Quatrain of Seven Steps". As the story goes, Cao Zhi had to write this poem quickly while under the threat that he would be killed by his brother if he failed. In some way there was a parallel, as I too was working under the pressure of time in an exchange program with Hyun Suk Seo from South Korea, who challenged me to develop a VR piece in a short period of time. It was also a metaphor for the pandemic, because the virus created a betrayal of sisterhood in both private and public spheres. The structure of the film thus took on a series of seven scenarios, played by seven performers.

UMB   The Seven Step Verse (2022) is predominantly occupied with Singapore's modernist architecture — what is your interest in that?

ER   The film is the latest development in my research and documentation on the aftereffects of modernism, and the spectrality caused by urbanization. In this instance, I observed the modernist shopping malls of Singapore, such as People's Park Complex, Golden Mile Tower, and Sim Lim Tower. They are faded monuments of the city's modernist but also social vision and are now occupied primarily by maid agencies or shop owners from other Southeast Asian countries, key players of the foreign workforce behind Singapore's progress. I adapted clothes for the performers in the styles and gestures of these workers, and we camouflaged ourselves as cleaning ladies in overalls colored in the same hues as Sim Lim Tower and 'invaded' the malls. As the 360° camera is still quite unknown to people, we were able to shoot in public without being noticed.

UMB   VR is a relatively new format and just starting to attract attention among filmmakers. What do you see as the possibilities of VR, and does it enable you to deepen your investigation of spaces? Or is it just a different way to approach space through film for you?

ER   Technology always formulates a new creative situation for artmaking, not the other way around. Cinema is a technological art to begin with — and it inaugurated new modes of thought and sensory engagement. I think that using VR technology demands a more performative approach, as the camera is stable and shows 360° views, so you have to make something happen around it in some way.

At the same time, the sonic element plays a major role in creating an immersive scenario. Sound, which is not recorded at the same time, then adds a new or even dissonant layer of textual meaning to the film. This technology is very theatrical in nature; we don't 'watch' a VR film, instead we experience it. VR invites viewers into a common playground to interact and to travel without physical displacement.

JMB Returning to the idea of walking in the city, or walking the city in The Seven Step Verse (2022), how would you describe your practice of artistic research in your film?

ER For this work, I was inspired by Georges Perec[1], who suggests walking through a street and reading everything you can, from advertisements, to billboards, to street names. Often encountered in physical spaces, these texts are now rendered in an embodied, virtual environment. This film is thus a practice of situated cinema. Where situated knowledge is knowledge production embedded in concrete historical, cultural, and linguistic context. Situated cinema is cinematic technology's inscription on the world. Knowledge is always produced through an individual subjectivity, and likewise, performativity in cinema stages a world of personal identification for communal experience. It is ultimately a transformative act, one that enables you to know the private world collectively.

NOTES

1   George Perec, *Species of Spaces and Other Pieces*, ed. and trans. by John Sturrock (London: Penguin Classics, 1997)

Double Vision: China from the Outside-In

——Itty Abraham

Xi Jinping's arrival at the pinnacle of power of the People's Republic of China a decade ago was accompanied by a new ideological vision: the China Dream. Eschewing earlier leadership cautions of 'hiding strength' and 'biding time,' Xi made clear that he was not willing to wait any longer — China had arrived and was looking to take its place as a world power and peer to the United States. The China Dream, William Callahan explains, is a complex imaginary[1]. It looks back — reminding the world that China is the oldest unbroken civilization, while also seeking to overcome past injustices and humiliations — as well as forward, proposing that the ongoing 'rejuvenation' of the Chinese nation will lead to national perfection and restore the Middle Kingdom to global pre-eminence. Yet for all the kinetic force of Chinese exceptionalism, Callahan argues, the China Dream also carries with it profound doubt — expressed as 'patriotic worrying' — an extended uncertainty that wonders if the nation and its resources are still adequate to fulfill the China Dream.

For the rest of the world, China's arrival as a world power under Xi was best captured by the Belt and Road Initiative (BRI). The BRI took shape as an extraordinarily ambitious plan to build transport and infrastructural connectivity across multiple continents, joining China, Central Asia, Southeast Asia, East Africa, the Middle East and Western Europe in a modern reconstruction of the old Silk Road. This included land routes to the west as well as sea paths linking new and old ports built on the islands and littoral of the Indian Ocean. These Belts and Roads cannot be seen in isolation from the parallel effort to create an alternative set of multilateral institutions — most prominently the Chinese-led Asian Infrastructure Investment Bank, Shanghai Cooperation Organization, and BRICS group of countries — centered on Beijing. Behind these financial and political institutions was the intent to lay the foundations of a new world order, aimed at replacing the post-war system centered on Washington. Taken to the limit, these China-centric projects lay claims to new universal standards and rules.

A narrative of China as a mobilized nation and a project of global dominance, coupled with the always-present mysteries of what China *really* wants and how the nation and its proxies, perceived as 'Orientals', were *thought* to want, provided a means for the Pentagon and Washington think-tanks to proclaim a new threat to American global hegemony. A new Cold War was underway, even as western corporations from Apple to Wal-Mart made a beeline for the PRC to set up cheap manufacturing hubs.

Given the ever-escalating *Sturm und Drang* on the global stage, it has become increasingly hard to see past the noise. This is where the work of filmmaker Ella Raidel becomes so important. Raidel's films over the last decade, *A Pile of Ghosts* (2021), *Double Happiness* (2014), and *SUBVERSES China in Mozambique* (2011), range widely across Chinese urban landscapes in transition and, importantly, go beyond the relatively familiar — Beijing, Shenzhen, and Shanghai — to include Mozambique and Austria as Chinese spaces. Hers are accounts of a shifting frontier, not a territorial edge as conventionally understood, but a frontier nonetheless: variously urban, international, historical, and temporal. Taken together, these films offer a vivid vantage point from which to assess and to understand the gaps and contradictions within an increasingly over-heated geopolitical echo chamber. These films join mediation with meditation, offering visual and sonic commentaries on the China Dream and the Belt and Road Initiative from the outside-in. Collectively, they offer a kind of double vision — compelling glimpses into the absences and silences drowned out by the shrill pitch of national slogans and international anxieties. In Raidel's steady gaze, and framed by the sounds and sights of building shells and churned-up earth, dreams become nightmares, futures are cast as ruins, the present is composed of promises, histories become disjointed, and geography takes on the guise of the fantastic.

The most conventional — by which I mean internationally familiar — account of China today comes from furthest away. *SUBVERSES China in Mozambique* (2011) is a film about China's much-discussed investments in sub-Saharan Africa. Set in Mozambique, the film offers a variety of perspectives on foreign investment from the bottom-up. The film begins with what we come to realize as a Raidel signature, first the sound and then the image of a Chinese man talking against a backdrop of new high-rise buildings and ongoing construction. The film takes in panoramic views of high-prestige projects, notably the international airport and the national stadium, and includes documentary accounts of Chinese supervisors and Mozambican workers. We get to see this latter encounter at a rare out critical moment in the relationship of boss and worker, namely, payday — one of the most disturbing sequences of the film.

Many of the visual segments in *SUBVERSES* are compelling but not to be surprised. The Chinese projects are huge, shiny and seem destined to be incomplete monuments to unequal bilateral engagement; the Chinese labor force lives in enforced segregation from the local community; their bosses enjoy a Maputo nightlife that is a simulacrum of the karaoke bars in the provincial towns they probably come from; and Chinese supervisors verbally abuse their Mozambican work force and try not to pay them their full salaries through aggression and bureaucratic misdirection. Exploitation is the fairly obvious subtext here. The African continent is presented as pure potential, and here, Chinese capital is just the latest foreign arrival to take advantage of Mozambique's natural resources and the equally natural venality of its politicians.

That is not all: Interspersed in these familiar accounts are staged portraits of Chinese and African men in the workplace. These are not brief or passing shots: The camera waits, forcing us to look closely at their postures and expressions. An uncanny kind of intimacy emerges as the distances between these uniformed and helmeted bodies appears to shrink, temporarily. We get a hint that the Chinese supervisor is only powerful in Mozambique; while back home, perhaps, he is not that different from his African counterpart.

Another kind of narrative interruption occurs when we encounter an older Chinese businessman. Sitting in an extraordinarily cluttered office in a typical grocery-cum-dry goods shop that sells everything a customer might need in small and affordable quantities, and speaking in fluent Portuguese, the man reminds us that the Chinese presence in Mozambique is not new. During the phases of decolonization in the African continent, China supported the freedom struggles of many African states. Most memorably, China built a railroad from Tanzania to Zambia in order to break the economic stranglehold of transport networks that tied Zambian copper to the ports of apartheid South Africa. Mozambique's long running and violent freedom struggle was also supported by China. This older businessman seems different from the entrepreneurs we have encountered thus far. "I am the last of a

kind," he says, wistfully invoking memories of others like him who have now retired or passed away.

This account of the Chinese businessman is an indication that the Chinese presence in Mozambique is not only new but has also become very different. The last of the small traders marks the frontier between an older and a newer China: the former, small in scale and unorganized, while the latter, massive and strategic. The former is constituted by adventurous families looking for economic opportunity, the latter is a coalition of state and private capital hoovering up natural resources and planting the flag wherever possible. We do not discover what Mozambicans think of the older traders, but we are told in no uncertain terms — notably, in eloquent bursts of rapping meter — that the new Chinese are neo-colonial. They are just the latest in a long line of outsiders who have taken advantage of Africa's wealth of resources to enrich themselves, at the expense of its local people.

Far from sunny and dusty Maputo, *A Pile of Ghosts* (2021) begins with dampness, mist and cold. Initially, we seem to be watching a remake of Jia Zhangke's memorable film, *The World* (2004). We see full-size recreations of the Parthenon, Sphinx, and Eiffel Tower being constructed, but this is not a feature film about young migrants working in an urban theme park. Instead, *A Pile of Ghosts* can be described as a meditation on the ruins that are simultaneously preconditions and aftermath to the transformations of urban China.

Ruins index both what was there before and what might take their place. They mark past histories and point to a future in the making. It is impossible not to think of Walter Benjamin in this context, especially his critical reading of the ruin and its relation to allegory: "Allegories are, in the realm of thought, what ruins are in the realm of things."[2] For Benjamin, the ruin as fragment was a means to counter the symbolism of the aesthetic object by proliferating its possible meanings. In *A Pile of Ghosts*, we are led to reflect on the allegory represented by the ruin of the Swallow Hotel that dominates the latter half of this film.

We meet the only inhabitant of the Swallow Hotel as he is dressing for the day. His surroundings are faded. The contrast between his dapper Western clothing and his fastidious yet mournful demeanor are striking. We wonder who he is and where he is going. We are yet to discover that he lives in a ruin, his childhood home, still filled with memorabilia of past lives we can only imagine. He watches the black and white film *Waterloo Bridge* (1940) on a small television monitor obsessively. A tragic melodrama of war, loss, and love, *Waterloo Bridge* is all about what might have been. Its turning points are built around miscommunication and misunderstandings among people without history; how powerful outside forces intervene into the private lives of individuals who must cope with them as best as they can.

A young woman appears at the closed door of the hotel. She claims to have booked a room at the hotel, an unlikely story. We watch the relationship between the two slowly take shape without being sure where it might lead. At one point we discover that we are watching a story adapted from the audition of the actor playing the only resident of the Swallow Hotel. Raidel has blurred the lines between documentary and narrative feature, and as a result the real and the imagined have been turned inside out. If *Waterloo Bridge* is the allegory — we imagine it must be — then this story-within-the-film can only end badly. Is it about the ruin of the Swallow Hotel, a victim of the remorseless drive to build a modern and urban China? Is it about a vanishing past that no one remembers? Is the Swallow House a sign of resistance: a 'nail house' that refuses to give in to the flood of cement and concrete and noise and dust that engulfs the film and indeed the country? Or, most simply, is it about waiting for something to happen?

The film does not try to answer these questions, leaving us unsettled in the effort to find coherence where there can be none. What does not leave the viewer, however, are the many still portraits of workers in incomplete buildings, sometimes just sitting alone and looking away, never minding the camera, at other times talking and playing with each other, somehow able to share their bare lives without obvious hostility or rancor. *A Pile of Ghosts* gives us glimpses of the silent and invisible: pasts that are still present, lives that have no futures, and futures that are built on imaginaries of elsewhere.

For China to take over the world, as the doomsayers proclaim, it must have a distinct vision. The China Dream, couched in sweeping, confident, yet vague language interspersed with powerful slogans

urging the nation forward, stands in for this vision. It is taken as proof by domestic and international audiences that Beijing is making a claim to world domination. For those who remain skeptical, they are told to visit today's China to marvel at its super-highways, high-speed railways, immaculately efficient airports, and seaports, and everywhere, tall and impressive buildings. If the visitor from the impoverished Global South is left speechless, the Euro-American tourist is shocked, impressed, even awed: All at once their historically famous homelands seem dull and backward. There can only be one conclusion: This is what the future looks like, and it speaks Mandarin.

Double Happiness (2014) disturbs this narrative and conclusion. This film is about the physical reproduction of a picturesque Austrian lakeside village — Hallstatt — in the center of a massive real estate development in southern China's Guangdong province. A meticulously recreated Hallstatt — including the Alpine Lake it overlooks — has become the spatial center and visual calling card of the real estate project. According to the building plan, this showpiece is to be surrounded by expensive houses that draw heavily on middle-European architectural motifs such as gables and steeply vaulted roofs, amidst tree-filled gardens. Behind the luxury homes are rows of high-rise buildings where less fortunate consumers could be associated with this imported lifestyle, albeit at a distance. Guangdong province is of course one of the earliest centers of China's remarkable economic boom, making its residents wealthy and sending land prices skyrocketing. To stand out in this crowded real estate landscape is not easy. The decision to recreate a UNESCO World Heritage site from Europe allowed the company to claim a singular uniqueness and novelty it could share with lucky consumers.

From an architectural standpoint, to copy a structure or design from elsewhere is hardly uncommon. To copy is even a kind of homage. The proof of the appeal of particular buildings is to see them replicated around the world. The modern skyscraper, now found around the world, but first built in Chicago and New York, is a case in point. Or consider Werner Herzog's *Fitzcarraldo* (1982), a film about a man's obsession. It takes its cue from the decision to build a replica of the Paris Opera in Manaus, an Amazonian city that was the hub of the global rubber boom in the 19th century. If it is hard to imagine traveling o Manaus to see its opera house, consider going to Buenos Aires instead, which hosts a smaller scale copy of the same Paris Opera. These structures may be in Latin America, but Paris is the reference point. These copies acquire their resonance by seeking association with the purported qualities of the "original" — sophistication, elegance, wealth, and ultimately, modernity.

By contrast, traditional Japanese temples that are described as being hundreds of years old are often recently built replicas of the original. Although, strictly speaking, these structures are copies, it is not considered unusual or a loss of authenticity to rebuild "traditional" wooden structures repeatedly, as long as the original design is maintained, and methods of building do not deviate from the past. Reproduction, in this context, is a mark of how important and socially valuable these temples are. In other words, a copy is not always a copy. We are, in turn, left confused: Is the original diminished by the copy? Or does the original acquire even more importance as something worthy of copying?

Double Happiness plays with these questions and their underlying conceit. Visually, the film makes it hard to tell where we are: Are we in Austria or China, looking at a small-scale replica, a builder's model, an advertising banner, the original village, or its visual reproduction? Raidel repeatedly and deliberately blurs the lines between the "real" Hallstatt and its multiple replicas, small and large, throughout the film. She takes full advantage of the camera's ability to lure us into thinking we know the real, only to show us that we are unable to distinguish the original from its copies. It is only when the camera pulls back to show the audience the edges of the frame that we realize what we were looking at, reminding us how easily we misread the visual truths apparently confirmed by fine-grained details. We are left disoriented; the net effect is to drive home the point that from the standpoint of the camera's gaze there may be little to distinguish between original and copy. Again, Walter Benjamin is invoked, but with a difference. This time around, his famous essay on "mechanical reproduction" is the reference point. The fabled authentic aura of the original work of art is left by the visual wayside, thanks to the industrial guile of the digital camera.

If the audience is led to question its ability to tell the difference between copy and the original, confusion is also rampant among the residents of Hallstatt, but differently. Local reactions range from outrage to being upset, but mostly come across as bemused, unsure of what exactly has taken place and how to think about it. Outrage for some comes from being copied without permission, even as the "theft" was carried out quite openly. One of the Chinese designers spent weeks in the heritage hotel that overlooks the central square, getting the physical details of the building as close to the original as possible. The hotel's owner remembers being puzzled and suspicious why someone would spend so much time sitting in the hotel lobby, "working" while on holiday. She could not imagine what this work would lead to. Yet, in the end, we also find that she has signed a contract with a Chinese firm to make new furniture when she decides to renovate her heritage hotel. The mayor of Hallstatt, accompanied by a small brass ensemble and television cameras, travels to Guangdong to take part in the formal inauguration of the real estate development. He is torn between the explicit compliment paid to his hometown and the quality of the Chinese copy. It leads him and others in the Austrian village to turn inward and to question themselves. Copying has disturbed their emotional foundations. The residents of Hallstatt now see themselves differently. Encountering a copy of their home far from home has made them reflexively insecure. Only the brass band seems unperturbed.

Looking beyond the real estate marketing ploy, understanding the Chinese decision to copy an Austrian village is not easy. Looking to the West for inspiration and validation has long been considered the mark of a colonial mindset, both in China and across the Global South. The China Dream is explicitly a repudiation of Western hegemony and global control, both reminder and paean to the Chinese nation to imagine itself as an independent civilizational power. Yet learning from the Western historical experience and its technologies have been critical to China's efforts to define its place in the world and its possible futures, going back to the discussions on "Mr. Science and Mr. Democracy" a century ago[4]. This ambivalence is often ignored. For many outside observers, the China Dream is little more than the latest expression — and confirmation — of a resurgent and belligerent China. It is far easier to pay attention to Xi Jinping's consolidation of power at the recently concluded 20th Party Congress than to grapple with the ambivalences that are products of the contemporary Chinese pursuit of economic development and cultural modernity.

It is against this intellectual inertia that Ella Raidel's work over the last decade becomes so useful. All three of the films discussed in this essay go behind and beyond these single-track images of a dangerous Chinese behemoth. We come to realize that the very success of China's economic transformation — an extraordinary and world-historical achievement by any standard — has led to a deep social ambivalence, expressed in different ways. "Patriotic worrying," to return to Callahan's reading of the China Dream, is another symptom of this ambivalence.

A Pile of Ghosts and *Double Happiness* work respectively through feelings of loss and ruin on the one hand, and the continuing allure of the foreign, on the Other. Taken together they make the future — the China Dream — a vision of doubt rather than confidence. 'All of China is a theme park,' one commentator says, and 'You can find any place in China,' begging the question of what remains Chinese in this pell-mell chase to build without stopping. We see young Chinese couples dressed up in wedding finery taking pictures against exotic landscapes whose whole point is that they are physically far from China: even poses in military uniforms and pigtails evoking the Communist Party's struggle against Japanese imperialists and Guomindang nationalists are little more than cosplay. The theme park that is modern China gets scripted as a Potemkin landscape, little more than an outdoor set made ready for WeChat selfies.

Taken together, Raidel's films are moving commentaries that help us see past the ceaseless sounds of bulldozers, earthmovers and welding guns that over-determine familiar visions of China. Just as China appears to have arrived, the idea of China starts slipping away, absent a remembered past and filled with borrowed futures from other places. What remains are haunting portraits of exhausted workers, the detritus of construction, an antechamber of forgotten memories. These are films of human ruins, of ghosts inhabiting a spirit world outlined in points of orange and yellow set against a palette of grays and browns.

NOTES

1   William A. Callahan, *China Dreams: 20 Visions of the Future* (Oxford: Oxford University Press, 2013)

2   Naomi Stead, "The Value of Ruins: Allegories of Destruction in Benjamin and Speer," in *Form/Work: An Interdisciplinary Journal of the Built Environment*, no. 6 (October 2003): 51-64 (4).

3   Walter Benjamin, *Illuminations*, ed. and with an introduction by Hannah Arendt, trans. Harry Zohn (New York: Schocken Books, 1969)

4   Hui Wang, "The Fate of 'Mr. Science' in China: The Concept of Science and its Application in Modern Chinese Thought," in *Formulations of Colonial Modernity in East Asia*, ed. by Tani Barlow (Durham: Duke University Press, 1997)

Ghost Infrastructu-reality

—— Yu Weiying

China's "ghost cities" lie in the shadow of contemporary urban infrastructure. With their distinct, empty spaces, these ghost cities, in turn, generate a subtractive space — a shadow — that lies as a backdrop against the progressive fullness of urbanization. In doing so, this subtractive space of urban infrastructure, constructed from replicas, demolition, and contemporary ruins, narrates a poetic desire for a space that lies in between reality and fantasy. Here, and in a similar vein, Ella Raidel's essay film, *A Pile of Ghosts* (一窟鬼, 2021), portrays a ghost "infrastructureality" in its presentation of the demolition of space, *shanzhai* architecture (copied buildings), and abandoned high-rise buildings. Where contemporary urban infrastructure grows and progresses beyond the imaginable, it also inevitably reshapes a contemporary man-made ghost of reality — a ghost "infrastructureality".

The global capital in housing investment is a reflection of China's cultural capital — a capital built upon the high-rise buildings that fill its modern cities, and its numerous miniature theme parks that are not only modeled after Western-style architecture but intended to be replicas of various Western tourist destinations as well. Where the former — its high-rise buildings — are concrete spaces meant to occupy, fill, and shape the city's urban infrastructure, the latter alludes to a spectacle and appropriation of the West, and reveals China's deep-seated desire to be a part of, and within the shared, global space inspired by the West and its supposed sense of modernity, a space it was resolutely left out from. In contrast, and instead of 'filling' the city, the subtractive spaces of China's ghost cities and their demolition opens speculative spaces that form the backdrop of capitalist spatial product and contemporary urban infrastructure.

These ghost cities are the primary subject of Raidel's film, *A Pile of Ghosts*, which is translated in Chinese as *Yi ku Gui* 一窟鬼. The title is taken from a *huaben* (话本, storytelling or script) in the Song dynasty (960–1276), *West Mountain, A Pile of Ghosts* 西山一窟鬼, of which the folk story tells the tale of a scholar who was wed to a ghost wife. As the film captures contemporary ghosts in a sense of global cultural fantasy, this up-to-date Chinese ghost story is haunted by westernization, capitalism, and urbanization. Going further, spatially and linguistically speaking, the word *ku* 窟 in Chinese is used in a historical context to refer to Buddhist caves such as *Mogao Ku* 莫高窟, or in a contemporary context to *Pinmin Ku* 贫民窟, which refers to slums, and urban residential areas that are highly populated by impoverished and marginalized people. However, Raidel's *A Pile of Ghosts* is not associated with any of these two contexts, but instead with an infrastructural space meant for and embraced by various "ghosts". This infrastructural space is one that is formulated by a man-made ghost of urban reality and takes form in three parts in Raidel's film: *Shanzhai*'s miniature theme park; numerous unoccupied high-rise building complexes; as well as housing demolition.

In the powerful flow of capital that fuels the process of constructing, and later demolishing urban infrastructure, the spatial product manifests itself in a visual and performative form in Raidel's film. The first five minutes of the film feature replicas of world-famous landmarks in Chinese theme parks, including the Eiffel Tower in Paris and the Parisian-style architecture of *Tianducheng* 天都城 in Hangzhou, the Sphinx in Egypt and The Parthenon in Athens in Lanzhou New Area, as well as the unfinished Disney-esque castle in the abandoned Wonderland Amusement Park in Beijing. Serving only as a backdrop or a display, or at most a contemporary means of earning capital, the infrastructure of *shanzhai* architecture functions as nothing more than an imitation of a visual and spatial experience of temporality. These constructions of *shanzhai* architecture can only grow increasingly distant from the everyday reality they can only wish to recreate. Here, the immiscible nature of the spectacle of tourism with the physical force of labor — felt ever so strongly especially with the country's unfinished and later abandoned projects — highlights the contradiction between China's "visual utopia" and its dismal reality. Instead of the concrete fulfillment of a promised future, the "visual utopia" in post-socialist China is characterized by a spectacle of shared spatial production, which signifies the desire for social and global mobility, as well as cultural capital.[1]

The subject of Raidel's film shifts to China's scores of unoccupied high-rise building complexes, in which the subtractive spaces of urban infrastructure — ghost infrastructureality — manifest themselves in. What initially appears to be well-developed real estate planning is quickly revealed to be far-fetched and a ruse, as the reality of realtors who market these buildings and their incomplete infrastructure, as well as the migrant construction workers who toil through the hard labor of building them, are brought to the forefront — they are ultimately part of the infrastructureality that fails to fulfill the concrete visions of the "promising future" that capital promotes. Raidel's film parallels this reality of realtors and construction workers with a conversation that takes place between a realtor and a potential client in front of a blank green screen. As the blank green screen symbolizes the illusive future delineated by the real estate industry, this conversation is likewise both shadowy and speculative — it is, after all, acted out, almost as if a play of sorts. With the subsequent monologue by a prospective realtor doing her job interview further reinforcing the performative reality that is shaped by global capitalism, the interplay between documentation and reality, fiction and performance in Raidel's film acknowledges the ghosts birthed from China's ghost infrastructureality as well.

The last section of *A Pile of Ghosts* is centered on The Swallows Hotel 燕子旅馆 and its owner, Charles. The hotel, first opened in April 4, 1984 in Chongqing by Charles' parents, has since become a "nail-house" 钉子户 situated in the last shanty town of the city, and sits on a plot of land surrounded by the demolished debris of old houses. Haunted by a number of memories and fantasies relating to The Swallows Hotel, Charles refuses to move, and his adamant resistance to the demolition of the hotel reflects his fear of losing the sense of personal identity and spatial history attached to it. The reality of the hotel's impending demolition conjures Charles' affection for his beloved classic Hollywood film, *Waterloo Bridge* (1940), which is also one of his mother's favorites. This, coupled with the emergence of a girl in Charles' everyday life, and who also visits The Swallows Hotel, intertwines fantasy and reality, as the tragic romance of *Waterloo Bridge* infiltrates Charles' day-to-day life, roving with him across the city's infrastructural spaces. Here, Charles' experience, and his unyielding hold on The Swallows Hotel as a marker of personal identity and spatial history highlights the pervasive, urban syndrome of demolition: just as The Swallows Hotel lies suspended in a city of ruins, so does the love story in his imagination whose ending remains suspended — what is left is a haunting narrative of the ghost of urbanization, or "a fiction of capitalism" that can only exist in the in-betweens of fantasy and reality.

Crucial to this narrative of the ghost of urbanization is the pervasive, subtractive space that converges across the private, urban,

and industrial landscape. This is most prominent in the transition from the scene in which Charles and the girl lie silently on the bed in a room at The Swallows Hotel to a one-and-a-half-minute shot of oil pumpjacks working rhythmically in the open landscape of Yumen (Gansu province), all with its soundscape intertwined with Teresa Teng's song, *Reminiscing the Past*, all of which alludes to what Raidel terms as an "imagined sex scene". Here, the power of this subtractive space does not only manifest in the demolition of China's artificial, abandoned infrastructure — it also redirects our focus to an Earth heading towards human-centered disability. Considering how cities are the most powerful in their configuration and visualization of the Anthropocene to transform the Earth[2], then the infrastructural space of real estate, industrial production, and global capitalism leads us to the Capitalocene as termed by Jason W. Moore. Ghost infrastructureality, in this case, is not an accidental counterpart of capitalist urbanization, but instead emerges as an inevitable yet discursive power from the abundance and eventual abandonment of spatial production in the time of the Anthropocene.

However, where the Anthropocene was conceived as a geological term used to capture the age and dominance of human activities on and throughout the Earth, Donna J. Haraway, in response, coins the Chthulucene over the Anthropocene, arguing that we should instead turn to speculative fabulation to tell alternative stories of the Earth that go far beyond its lauded narratives.[3] In the spirit of the Chthulucene, then, *A Pile of Ghosts* characterizes the Anthropocene as a period of ghosts — ghosts of infrastructure. More than just empty and inert materialization, the Anthropocene in this case is full of left-out and leftover remnants of discursive practices that arise from some, if not all forms of capitalist planning. In fact, the fabulation of infrastructure as a ghost, or as ghosts, echoes Haraway's notions of spatial narration — the narrative crafted as urban infrastructure is fabulated as a reality of ghosts in the Anthropocene, or rather, and returning to the term, "ghost infrastructureality". After all, the infrastructural space does not demand narration to begin with, nor does the space instruct itself with a subtractive impulse to go backwards in history or ahead in decay — in this reality, its ghosts can only find their place in the landscape of the Anthropocene, crafted by the expanding infrastructure of ghost cities and abandoned spaces.

It is interesting to note that many of these ghost cities can also be experienced virtually as urban exploration-themed visual content, which circulate widely on popular Chinese social media platforms such as the video-sharing website *Bilibili* 哔哩哔哩 (or B site), where viewers' comments can, in fact, be overlaid on the videos in real time, as well as *Little Red Book* 小红书 (an Instagram-like application). Rather than serving as dark tourist locations historically associated with manmade catastrophe or death, this unofficial and temporary visual archive of ghost cities can also be thought of as a patchwork of infrastructureality in the Anthropocene, crafting their own sort of narrative to the ghosts that reside in these spaces.

Raidel's ongoing art-based research project, *Of Haunted Spaces*, which includes *A Pile of Ghosts*, is a visual "cartography" of global capitalism in contemporary China. More specifically, it showcases multiple Chinese ghost cities as a backdrop to the performance of global capitalism. In turn, *Of Haunted Spaces* contextualizes a concept of 'ruin' in relation to Chinese ghost cities. Where Art historian Wu Hung has traced this "ruin culture" from ancient to contemporary China, and in particular, the urban ruins that arise from contemporary Chinese artistic practices, Raidel's *A Pile of Ghosts* presents us with a third kind of ruin beyond "monumental industrial ruins and intimate urban ruins"[4] — that which exists in the ruins of ghost cities, and from which infrastructure and urbanization materialize as empty spaces, ghosts that accumulate within a nonproductive reality.

As we return to Raidel's translated title, *Yi ku Gui* 一窟鬼, it is interesting to note that the further deconstruction — demolition, even — of the character *ku* 窟 reveals that right in the middle of the word is the part *shi* 尸, which refers to a dead body. In many ways, the infrastructure of the character *ku* 窟 seems to shelter these dead bodies — these ghosts — who are deprived of and from space (demolition) or trapped within them (in empty cities). Raidel's *A Pile of Ghosts* is ultimately a response to Haraway's call for a movement towards the Chthulucene, in its narration of the numerous subtractive spaces that make up the Anthropocene's infrastructureality.

NOTES

1   Lu Pan. "The Kitschy, the *Shanzhai*, and the Ugly:
    Creating Architectural Utopia in Contemporary
    Chinese Cities," in *Politics and Aesthetics of
    Creativity: City, Culture, and Space in East Asia*,
    ed. by Lu Pan, Heung Wah Wong, and Karin
    Ling-fung Chau (Los Angeles: Bridge 21
    Publications, 2015), 153-182.

2   James Lovelock, *Novacene: The Coming Age
    of Hyperintelligence*. (London: Penguin Books,
    2020), 71.

3   Donna Haraway, *Staying with the Trouble:
    Making Kin in the Chthulucene*. (Durham, North
    Carolina: Duke University Press, 2016), 51-57.

4   Hung Wu, *A Story of Ruins: Presence and Absence
    in Chinese Art and Visual Culture*. (Princeton:
    Princeton University Press, 2012), 241.

Ella Raidel is an artist and filmmaker. In her interdisciplinary practice, she focuses on the socio-cultural aspects of globalization, urbanization, and the politics of images with her writings and research on cinema aesthetics. She is the co-editor of *Altering Archives, The Politics of Memory in Sinophone Cinemas and Image Culture* with Peng Hsiao-yen, and published the book, *Subversive Realitäten: Tsai Ming-Liang und seine Filme* after her doctoral study. Raidel's works have been featured in biennials and exhibitions, such as Taipei Biennial (2016), Guangzhou Triennial (2015), Bi-City Architecture Biennale Hong Kong (2015), Manchester Asian Triennial (2008), and more, and were presented at film festivals, including IFFR Film Festival Rotterdam, CPH: DOX Copenhagen Documentary Film Festival, DOK Leipzig, Hot Docs Canada, Chicago Film Festival, Singapore Film Festival, and more.

She received the Outstanding Artist Award for Documentary and Fiction Film from the Austrian Federal Ministry of Arts and Culture (2022), and the Award of Excellence from the Federal Ministry of Education, Science and Research Austria (2010) for her research work; she earned the senior postdoctoral fellowship from Elise Richter PEEK, Austrian Science Fund (2016–2019) and postdoctoral fellowship of Academia Sinica Taipei (2013–2014). Her film *A Pile of Ghosts* received the Award for Excellence, Image Forum Festival Tokyo (2022).

Based in Singapore, Taiwan, and Austria, she is now an Assistant Professor at ADM School of Art, Design and Media and WKWSCI Wee Kim Wee School of Communication and Information at NTU Nanyang Technological University Singapore.

Ute Meta Bauer is the Founding Director of NTUCCA Singapore, and Professor, School of Art, Design and Media, Nanyang Technological University. For more than three decades, Bauer has been a curator/co-curator of exhibitions and presentations, connecting contemporary art, film, video, and sound through transdisciplinary formats including *Documenta11*, the *3rd Berlin Biennale for Contemporary Art*, and the US Pavilion for the *56th Venice Biennale*, featuring eminent artist Joan Jonas. Recent co-edited books include *The Impossibility of Mapping (Urban Asia)* (NTU CCA Singapore/World Scientific Publishing, 2020) and *Place.Labour.Capital.* (NTU CCA Singapore/Mousse Publishing, 2018).

Itty Abraham is Professor in the School for the Future of Innovation in Society at Arizona State University. He specializes in the postcolonial politics of science and technology, especially in Asia and the Global South. His scholarship ranges from nuclear studies and international relations to refugees and cultural studies. He has taught at the National University of Singapore and University of Texas at Austin and was program director at the Social Science Research Council, New York.

Marlene Rutzendorfer is an architect and curator of film and architecture, among others at the Architekturzentrum Vienna, as well as the traveling architecture film festival *Movies in Wonderland*. Since 2012 she has been developing formats of architectural mediation and interactive urban research, participatory design, and construction of exhibition architectures with the platform for architecture *Wonderland*.

Yu Weiying is an independent curator, art writer, and researcher based in Hong Kong and San Francisco. She is a PhD candidate at the Hong Kong Polytechnic University, and her doctoral project concerns infrastructure space in China after 1949 and on a planetary scale. She has been organizing artist residency programs and overseeing exhibitions at the San Francisco Bay Area non-profit organizations. She worked as a 2020 Asia Collection Research Fellow at the Kadist Art Foundation.

IMAGE CREDITS

All images are copyright to Ella Raidel unless mentioned otherwise.

IMAGE INDEX

LOCATION REFERENCES

AUSTRIA

Hallstatt, 2012

Hallstatt is located in Upper Austria, Salzkammergut Region, and is a UNESCO World Heritage Site since 1997. The Alpine village became popular among East Asian tourists, when it was featured on the Korean TV series *Spring Waltz* (2006). The small town, with a population of 800, is confronted every year with an estimated one million tourists.

CHINA

Beigao (北皋), Beijing, 2011

From this desert of rubble, people are extracting bricks and recyclable materials. Rapid urbanization has erased old houses, neighbourhoods, and communities.

Chenzhuang Cultural Plaza (陈庄文化广场), Beijing, 2016

Wonderland Amusement Park, Chenzhuang Village (陈庄村), is an abandoned and never completed amusement park outside Beijing. The concrete castle is the last reminder of this demolished dreamland.

Chao Yang District (朝阳区), Beijing, 2017

Old villages are destroyed in favor of new developments, but their construction has not yet begun. The areas are surrounded by a wall and covered with green fabric mimicking grass. Traces of the old villages such as trees and roads are shimmering through the green fabric.

The Swallow Hotel (燕子旅馆), Chongqing (重庆), 2017–19

Charles is the owner of the Swallow Hotel in the hills of Chongqing overlooking the Yangtze River. The picturesque area is undergoing drastic changes; the area has been gentrified and local residents have to move out. Charles refuses to move, and the Swallow Hotel remains as a nail-house in a ruined landscape. Despite the transition, Charles is creating a world of his own from the fantasy of *Waterloo Bridge*, the Hollywood film.

Backstreet (后街) , Chongqing, 2019

Backstreet is the name and neon sign of a photo studio behind the area of the Swallow Hotel.

Hallstatt See (五矿·哈施塔特), 2012–13

Hallstatt See in Boluo (博罗), near Huizhou, was planned as a luxury real-estate project copied from the Austrian village of the same name. The landscape was transformed, the mountains were divided and reshaped to resemble the region of the Alps. The town became the stage for projecting the imagination of a life in Austria. It turned into a busy tourist attraction and backdrop for wedding photography and film shoots.

Xian Village (先村), Guangzhou (广州), 2017

The buildings are called "handshake-buildings" (握手楼), because the distance between them is so narrow that residents can shake hands from the windows. The urban villages are on the verge of disappearance due to the government's urban policy. Every day buildings are being demolished the lanes are being widened so the hand-shake is no longer possible.

Haiyang Urbanization (海洋), Yantai (烟台), 2016

High-rises along the coast, holiday resorts and hotels are built in great numbers and falling into ruins, and people may come once a year for summer break, while new projects are being constructed and waiting for their new owners.

Lanzhou New Area (兰州), Gansu (甘肃), 2017

Lanzhou New Area in Gansu Province, hundreds of mountains are being removed to build a new city. The advertisement renders the vision of a green garden landscape with 14 new universities with boulevards of eight lanes for traffic and transportation. Newly planted trees line the freshly paved avenues in what used to be a desert.

Lanzhou Silk Road Cultural Relics Park (丝绸之路文化遗产博览城), Lanzhou New Area (兰州新区), 2017

Excavators in their hundreds are flattening the mountains, and from afar they look like matchbox cars in a sandbox. The yellow loess looks soft, but these dunes are deformed by the ongoing construction. A huge Sphinx, the Parthenon and several other world monuments are being built as part of an amusement park. A theme park is a necessary facility of every new urban development in China.

Ordos (鄂尔多斯), 2013

Ordos, located in Inner Mongolia, China, means 'many palaces' and is a completely new city with a futuristic museum built by star architect Ma Yansong (马岩松). Arriving at the city at dusk in 2013 only a few lights were visible in a horizon of high rises. New ghost cities in China serve as the doorway to reveal the ever-growing scales and economic dimension of the neoliberal market in its most extreme.

Tianducheng (天都城), 2016

Tianducheng, located near Hangzhou, is a replica of Paris, complete with its own Eiffel Tower and Haussmannian-style buildings. The new urban space is haunted by hyper-urbanization, which has been offered by the government and the real estate market as a new way of dwelling.

Yumen (玉门), 2017

Yumen is an industrial city located in the hinterland of Jiayuguan (嘉峪关), in Gansu province. It was China's first oil well, drilled in 1939, and reached its peak production in 1959. However, since then, production has been declining. Recently, tens of thousands of residents were relocated 70 kilometers away to Yumen New Area, and the old Yumen has become a memorial site for state-owned industry.

MOZAMBIQUE

Estádio do Zimpeto, Stadium, Maputo, Mozambique, 2010

Maputo International Airport, Maputo, Mozambique, 2010

Shooting sites of *SUBVERSES China in Mozambique*, among other locations in Maputo, Mozambique are Estádio do Zimpeto, the football stadium and Maputo International Airport under construction, built with funds from the Chinese government and constructed by Anhui Foreign Economic Construction Group (AFECC).

Poetas D'Alma, Maputo, Mozambique, 2010

The Poetas D'Alma is a Slam Poetry Collective, based at the Mozambican-German Cultural Center (CCMA), Goethe-Zentrum Maputo.

FILM CREDITS

THE SEVEN-STEP VERSE
VR, 9 min., 2022

DIRECTOR AND PRODUCER	Ella Raidel
CINEMATOGRAPHER	Benjamin Seide
SOUND RECORDING	Vanessa Yip, Chua Xin Yun, Yang Haolin
SOUND DESIGN	Ross Adrian Williams
EDITOR	Benjamin Seide
COMPOSER	Ross Adrian Williams
PRODUCTION DESIGN	Ella Raidel
COLOR CORRECTION	Benjamin Seide
TITLE DESIGN	Benjamin Seide
PERFORMER	Nicole Phua, Veronyka Lau, Valerie Koon, Smiha Kapoor, Gladis Ng*
SUPPORTED BY	ARKO The Arts Council Korea/ International Arts Joint Fund/Korea-Singapore International Exchange Program, NTU Cohass Arts and Humanities Research Grant, ADM School of Art, Design, and Media
DISTRIBUTED BY	Lemonade Films Vienna

A PILE OF GHOSTS
70 min., 2021

DIRECTOR AND PRODUCER	Ella Raidel
KEY CAST	Yakira Cang, Yang Ke
EDITOR	Daniel Hui
CINEMATOGRAPHY	Djordje Arambasic, Karel Picha, Vincent Zheng
VISUAL EFFECTS	Benjamin Seide
COLOR GRADING	Junbin Chen
SOUND	Tong Zhang, Huawei Cheng
SOUND DESIGN	Sander Saarmets
ASSISTANT PRODUCER	Hongjohn Lin
EXECUTIVE PRODUCER	Ursula Wolschlager
SUPPORTED BY	The Austrian Science Fund (FWF), Federal Ministry Republic of Austria Arts and Culture, BKA — innovative film, Vienna Culture MA 7, Upper Austria Culture, NTU Singapore
DISTRIBUTED BY	Sixpackfilm Vienna

WE WILL ALWAYS HAVE PARIS
4 min., 2020

DIRECTOR AND PRODUCER	Ella Raidel
SOUND DESIGN	Sander Saarmets
SUPPORTED BY	Kunstuniversität Linz
DISTRIBUTED BY	Sixpackfilm Vienna

DOUBLE HAPPINESS
4 min., 2014

DIRECTOR AND PRODUCER	Ella Raidel
KEY CAST	Yakira Cang
PARTICIPANTS	Wu Wenyuan, Siegwulf Turek, Monika Wenger, MAD Architect Ma Yansong, Yansplan
EDITOR	Karina Ressler
CINEMATOGRAPHY	Martin Putz
MUSIC	Rudi Fischerlehner
SOUND	Wong Ka Ho
SOUND DESIGN	Matthias Kassmannhuber, Marco Zinz
SUPPORTIVE PRODUCER	Peter Janecek
SUPPORTED BY	Federal Ministry Republic of Austria Arts and Culture, BKA — innovative film, Vienna Culture MA 7, Upper Austria Culture
DISTRIBUTED BY	Sixpackfilm Vienna

CINEMA ISN'T I SEE, IT'S I FLY
min., 2013

DIRECTOR AND PRODUCER	Ella Raidel
CINEMATOGRAPHY	Ella Raidel
SKYDIVER	Fabian Raidel
SUPPORTED BY	Silhouette
DISTRIBUTED BY	Sixpackfilm Vienna

Crossing Europe Film festival Trailer 2013

PLAY LIFE SERIES
1 min., 2012

DIRECTOR AND PRODUCER	Ella Raidel
CINEMATOGRAPHY	Ella Raidel
MUSIC	Anselm C. Kreuzer, Hongjohn Lin
SUPPORTED BY	Supported by Federal Ministry Republic of Austria Arts and Culture; BMUKK
DISTRIBUTED BY	Sixpackfilm Vienna

Chicago International Film festival Trailer, 1 min., 2016

SUBVERSES CHINA IN MOZAMBIQUE
45 min., 2011

DIRECTOR AND PRODUCER	Ella Raidel
CINEMATOGRAPHY	Ella Raidel
EDITOR	Thomas Schneider, Ella Raidel
MUSIC	Matchume Zango
PERFORMER	Mestre Tchaka, Poeta Militar, Pha Teca-Teca
SUPPORTED BY	Upper Austria Culture, City of Linz Culture
DISTRIBUTED BY	Sixpackfilm Vienna

SLAM VIDEO MAPUTO
27 min., 2010

DIRECTOR AND PRODUCER	Ella Raidel
CINEMATOGRAPHY	Ella Raidel
SUPPORTED BY	City of Linz Culture, LinzExport
DISTRIBUTED BY	Sixpackfilm Vienna

In Cooperation with IFFR International Film Festival Rotterdam

Forget Africa programmed by Gertjan Zuilhof

About NTU Centre for Contemporary Art Singapore

A national research centre of Nanyang Technological University, the NTU Centre for Contemporary Art Singapore positions itself as a space for critical discourse and encourages new ways of thinking about Spaces of the Curatorial in Southeast Asia and beyond. It brings forth innovative and experimental forms of engagement artistic and curatorial practices that intersect the present and histories of contemporary art embedded in social-political spheres with other fields of knowledge.

Acknowledgement

Ella Raidel extends sincere gratitude to following individuals who have played a significant role in bringing this publication to fruition: Ute Meta Bauer, the editor, for her invaluable guidance and support; Itty Abraham, Marlene Rutzendorfer, and Yu Weiying for their thoughtful and engaged text contributions, Edda Hoefer and Hongjohn Lin for their expertise and insights.

Of Haunted Spaces: An Essay Film on Ghost cities was supported as Elise-Richter PEEK project by the Austrian Science Fund (FWF), Project Number: V 492-G24
https://www.hauntedspaces.net/
This publication is supported by NTU Nanyang Technological University Singapore, Starting Grant.

Federal Ministry
Republic of Austria
Arts, Culture,
Civil Service and Sport

The Films Of Ella Raidel
Of Haunted Spaces
Cinema, Heterotopias, And China's Hyperurbanization

EDITOR	Ute Meta Bauer
PROOFREADERS	Edda Hoefer, Han Pei Lin Kimberly
FINANCIAL DEPARTMENT	NTU management staff Lew Huey Shan, and Tan Wee Liang
DESIGNER	Studio SWELL
PRINTER	First Printers Pte. Ltd.
PUBLISHED BY	NTU Centre for Contemporary Art Singapore
ISBN	978-981-18-5893-2
DISTRIBUTED BY	NUS Press, National University of Singapore, AS3 #01-02, 3 Arts Link, Singapore 117569

NTU Centre for Contemporary Art Singapore

Gillman Barracks, Block 6, Lock Road, Singapore 108934
http://ntu.ccasingapore.org/

National Library Board, Singapore
Cataloguing in Publication Data

Names: Bauer, Ute Meta, editor.
Title: The films of ELLA RAIDEL, *Of Haunted Spaces*
Cinema, Heterotopias, and China's Hyperurbanization/edited by Ute Meta Bauer.
Description: Singapore: NTU Centre for Contemporary Art Singapore
Identifiers: ISBN: 978-981-18-5893-2
Subjects: The Films of Ella Raidel

NANYANG TECHNOLOGICAL UNIVERSITY